# PRAYERS OF THE NEW TESTAMENT

LYNNE
M. BAAB

8 STUDIES
FOR INDIVIDUALS
OR GROUPS

Life
Builder
Study

INTER-VARSITY PRESS
36 Causton Street, London SW1P 4ST, England
*Email: ivp@ivpbooks.com*
*Website: www.ivpbooks.com*



*Originally published in the United States of America in the LifeGuide® Bible Studies series in 2010 by InterVarsity Press, Downers Grove, Illinois*
*First published in Great Britain by Scripture Union in 2012*
*This edition published in Great Britain by Inter-Varsity Press 2019*

**British Library Cataloguing-in-Publication Data**
A catalogue record for this book is available from the British Library.

ISBN: 978–1–78359–829–8

Printed in Great Britain by Ashford Colour Press Ltd, Gosport, Hampshire

*Inter-Varsity Press publishes Christian books that are true to the Bible and that communicate the gospel, develop discipleship and strengthen the church for its mission in the world.*

*IVP originated within the Inter-Varsity Fellowship, now the Universities and Colleges Christian Fellowship, a student movement connecting Christian Unions in universities and colleges throughout Great Britain, and a member movement of the International Fellowship of Evangelical Students. Website: www.uccf.org.uk. That historic association is maintained, and all senior IVP staff and committee members subscribe to the UCCF Basis of Faith.*

# Contents

# Getting the Most Out of *Prayers of the New Testament*

A group of young adults gathers late on a Sunday night in a cathedral. They fill the pews, sprawl on the floor and sit with their backs against the enormous pillars that hold up the ornate ceiling. They are waiting to begin Compline (pronounced "COM•plin"), a simple worship service with only a few psalms and prayers, a Scripture reading, and a hymn. The huge cathedral organ will ring out with Bach's glorious tones at the end of the service.

Christians have been participating in Compline services for more than a thousand years. A brief prayer from Luke 2 is part of the service. It's a vivid prayer that comes from the heart of an old man, Simeon, who had been watching for God's salvation. When the infant Jesus is brought to the temple, Simeon is filled with certainty that here, at last, is God's salvation for the whole earth. With great joy, Simeon realizes he can now die at peace because of this baby's birth.

Simeon's prayer is only three verses long, but it has been repeated throughout many centuries in the Compline service. Numerous other prayers in the New Testament have also held a similar significant place of honor among Christians in many settings and over many years, such as Mary's prayer, Jesus' high priestly prayer and Paul's prayers in his letters.

In this guide, you are invited to study eight prayers in the New Testament that contain beautiful language and deep thoughts, evoking God's character and attributes with rich metaphors and powerful images. As you engage in this study, watch for the clear and vivid writing that makes these prayers express so much in only a few words.

In addition, watch for the ways you can grow in your own prayer life through studying these prayers. Perhaps this study will encourage you to open your Bible to one of these prayers at some point in the future and pray that prayer for yourself or someone you love. Or you may want to memorize one or more of these prayers so you can let their profound ideas and lovely language sink into your soul. If you memorize one, you can pray it in your car, in the middle of the night or in other situations when a Bible isn't handy. You might even want to rewrite one or more of the prayers, paraphrasing them so they apply more directly to your life or to the concerns of someone for whom you are praying.

Prayer is the invitation from God for us to draw near, and Jesus Christ has made it possible for us to do so. "For we do not have a high priest who is unable to sympathize with our weaknesses," wrote the author of Hebrews, "but we have one who has been tempted in every way, just as we are—yet was without sin. Let us then approach the throne of grace with confidence, so that we may receive mercy and find grace to help us in our time of need" (4:15-16).

We can draw near to God in every setting of our lives: in church, outdoors in nature, at the kitchen table, in front of a computer and in other everyday settings. These prayers from the New Testament will help us find new language for our prayers. They will open up fresh ideas of what to pray for. And they will help us approach God's wonderful throne of grace to find the mercy and grace we need to live joyful, obedient lives.

**Suggestions for Individual Study**

**1.** As you begin each study, pray that God will speak to you through his Word.

**2.** Read the introduction to the study and respond to the personal reflection question or exercise. This is designed to help you focus on God and on the theme of the study.

**3.** Each study deals with a particular passage so that you can delve into the author's meaning in that context. Read and reread the passage to be studied. The questions are written using the language of the New International Version, so you may wish to use that version of the Bible. The New Revised Standard Version is also recommended.

**4.** This is an inductive Bible study, designed to help you discover for yourself what Scripture is saying. The study includes three types of questions. *Observation* questions ask about the basic facts: who, what, when, where and how. *Interpretation* questions delve into the meaning of the passage. *Application* questions help you discover the implications of the text for growing in Christ. These three keys unlock the treasures of Scripture.

Write your answers to the questions in the spaces provided or in a personal journal. Writing can bring clarity and deeper understanding of yourself and of God's Word.

**5.** It might be good to have a Bible dictionary handy. Use it to look up any unfamiliar words, names or places.

**6.** Use the prayer suggestion to guide you in thanking God for what you have learned and to pray about the applications that have come to mind.

**7.** You may want to go on to the suggestion under "Now or Later," or you may want to use that idea for your next study.

### Suggestions for Members of a Group Study

**1.** Come to the study prepared. Follow the suggestions for individual study mentioned above. You will find that careful preparation will greatly enrich your time spent in group discussion.

**2.** Be willing to participate in the discussion. The leader of your group will not be lecturing. Instead, he or she will be encouraging the members of the group to discuss what they have learned. The leader will be asking the questions that are found in this guide.

**3.** Stick to the topic being discussed. Your answers should be based on the verses which are the focus of the discussion and not on outside authorities such as commentaries or speakers. These studies focus on a particular passage of Scripture. Only rarely should you refer to other portions of the Bible. This allows for everyone to participate in in-depth study on equal ground.

**4.** Be sensitive to the other members of the group. Listen attentively when they describe what they have learned. You may be surprised by their insights! Each question assumes a variety of answers. Many questions do not have "right" answers, particularly questions that aim at meaning or application. Instead the questions push us to explore the passage more thoroughly.

When possible, link what you say to the comments of others. Also, be affirming whenever you can. This will encourage some of the more hesitant members of the group to participate.

**5.** Be careful not to dominate the discussion. We are sometimes so eager to express our thoughts that we leave too little opportunity for others to respond. By all means participate! But allow others to also.

**6.** Expect God to teach you through the passage being discussed and through the other members of the group. Pray that you will have an enjoyable and profitable time together, but also that as a result of the study you will find ways that you can take action individually and/or as a group.

**7.** Remember that anything said in the group is considered confidential and should not be discussed outside the group unless specific permission is given to do so.

**8.** If you are the group leader, you will find additional suggestions at the back of the guide.

# 1

# A Prayer of Mary

## *Praising the Mighty One*

### *Luke 1:39-56*

What does praise look like and feel like for you? For me, it's often associated with music. I love to sing praise songs in a congregation, swaying in time to the strong rhythm of drums, guitars and other instruments. I love the old hymns just as much; a beautiful organ accompanying a well-loved hymn can lift my heart to God in a wonderful way. God's goodness and love feel powerful and real when music fills my heart.

I also find myself praising God when I hear a good story, particularly a story about God's unexpected and powerful intervention in someone's life. Sometimes those stories are local and close by: a friend describes an answer to prayer, or I hear someone tell a story in church about God's faithfulness in his or her life. Other times those stories come from far away. An email from a ministry organization tells about the difference a very small loan made in one woman's life in Ghana. Or a presentation about China tells how God miraculously worked among a group of Christians there. My heart lifts to God in praise and thanks.

GROUP DISCUSSION. In what settings do you find yourself praising God? What form does praise usually take for you?

PERSONAL REFLECTION. Write a prayer of praise. Base the prayer on God's action in your life, in the lives of family and friends, and around the world. As you write, think about God's actions throughout time as well. If you are unable to write a prayer of praise right now, write a prayer that expresses your willingness to grow in learning to praise God.

Mary, the mother of Jesus, praises God for his mighty power in her life and among people in need. Her song of praise encompasses the local and the global throughout all time and is a favorite New Testament prayer for many Christians. *Read Luke 1:39-56.*

---

**1.** List the extraordinary events described in these verses.

---

**2.** The word "blessed" is used four times in this passage. Who is called "blessed"?

What do you think the word "blessed" means?

**3.** In the first few lines of Mary's prayer, she focuses on God's work in her own life. Notice the names and characteristics of God Mary cites in verses 47 to 49. Why do you think she cites those particular names and characteristics of God?

---

**4.** What names and characteristics of God have you especially noticed lately?

---

**5.** In verse 50, Mary's focus shifts to include "those who fear him / from generation to generation." What do you think it means to fear God?

---

**6.** Why would fearing God be connected to God's mercy (v. 50)?

---

**7.** What reversals of roles or statuses does Mary attribute to God in verses 51 to 53?

**8.** Have you seen reversals like these in your life or in the lives of others you know? If so, describe the circumstances.

---

**9.** Reread verse 45. In what ways do Mary and her prayer exemplify the description in this verse of a blessed person?

---

**10.** Mary's prayer expresses her conviction that God is powerful and also willing to intervene in the lives of people who need help. How does this combination of attributes make you feel toward God?

---

**11.** Name some of the situations and people in your life that you need God to intervene powerfully for.

---

**12.** In what ways do you (or how can you start to) express your belief in both God's power and his willingness to intervene in our lives?

*Spend some time praising God for his power and love, and then pray for the people and situations where his power and love are needed.*

## Now or Later

As you begin this study guide, consider your desires and dreams for your prayer life. Spend some time reflecting on, journaling about or discussing the ways you would like to grow and develop your own prayer practices. What do you like about the way you pray, both alone and with others? What aspects of your current prayer life are not satisfying? In what ways would you like to grow in prayer? Spend some time praying about the role of prayer in your life, confessing your shortcomings to God, asking for God's guidance for ways to grow in prayer and telling God your dreams for your prayer life.

Psalms is often called "the prayer book of the Bible," and in this study each New Testament prayer is paired with a passage from Psalms that has some of the same themes. Read Psalm 145 twice, the first time to get an overview of what the psalm is about and the ways it mirrors Mary's prayer, and then the second time slowly, praying the words of the psalm as you read.

# 2

# Prayers of Simeon and Anna

## *Seeing God at Work*

### *Luke 2:22-38*

My two grandmothers couldn't have been more different, yet they were both powerful models for me of what it looks like to be a Christian in the later years of life. Nona, my father's mother, was one of the most peaceful, loving people I have ever met. She exuded enjoyment of God's good gifts in everyday life, and she always saw the best in people around her. Her joy and gratitude spilled over into prayers of praise for God's greatness and thankfulness for God's good gifts to her.

Grandma Katie, in contrast, was a person of goals and high standards, who always strove for excellence in everything she did. She read through the Bible cover to cover every year, prayed for missionaries and tithed even during the Depression when money was very tight. She modeled faithfulness to God in many ways, including a deep commitment to intercessory prayer for the great needs in the world.

Both of my grandmothers died the year I was thirty-three, and I often wonder what I would learn now if I could have just one more conversation with them. I'd like to ask Nona where her peace and joy came from. Were they rooted in her prayers of praise and thanks? I'd like to ask Grandma Katie what motivated her to strive for excellence and to read the Bible with such commitment. Were those characteristics connected to her commitment to intercessory prayer?

GROUP DISCUSSION. On a piece of paper, write the names of several older people who have been models for you, particularly in the area of prayer. Beside their names, list the character traits they modeled for you and note any ways those traits spilled over into their prayer life. Describe to the group one of those character traits and how the person modeled it.

PERSONAL REFLECTION. Spend some time thinking about the older people in your life who have been models for you, particularly in the area of prayer. Write out a prayer thanking God for the way they influenced you, and in the prayer ask for God's help to be a model to people who are younger than you.

Anna and Simeon in Luke 2 have been models of older age and wisdom for many Christians over the centuries. Their stories help us learn to be open to the Spirit when we pray. *Read Luke 2:22-38.*

---

**1.** Imagine you're walking closely behind Mary and Joseph after these events and overhear their conversation. What do you think they might say to each other or remark about as they leave the temple with Jesus?

**2.** What do we learn about Mary and Joseph from verses 22 to 24?

---

**3.** Luke describes Simeon as "righteous and devout" and says "the Holy Spirit was upon him" (v. 25). What do you think these characteristics look like as they're lived out in everyday life?

---

**4.** In what ways would you like the Holy Spirit to be more present in your life?

---

**5.** Paraphrase Simeon's prayer in verses 29 to 32 to express his main point.

---

**6.** What do you think is the significance of Simeon's inclusion of "all people" in his prayer (v. 31)?

---

**7.** Anna and her actions are described in verses 36 to 38. Compare and contrast the description of Anna with the words about Simeon in verses 25 to 28.

**8.** Describe some of the ways you would like to resemble Simeon and Anna.

---

**9.** The combination of obedience to God's word and openness to the Holy Spirit's guidance enabled Mary, Joseph, Simeon and Anna to experience this amazing moment. How do obedience to God and openness to the Spirit lay a foundation for prayer?

---

**10.** How have you seen obedience and openness to the Spirit work together in your life?

What would help you grow in these two areas?

---

**11.** When you look back on the past week, what can you see God doing?

*Spend some time praising and thanking God for his actions in your life during the past week.*

## Now or Later

Luke 1:57-79 records the events around the birth of John the Baptist, which are similar to Simeon and Anna's story; both involve God's miraculous action and a spoken prayer. The prayer of Zechariah, John the Baptist's father, is traditionally read during morning prayer because of the reference to the "rising sun" (v. 78). Read the whole passage, then focus on Zechariah's prayer and compare and contrast it with Simeon's prayer. Use parts of either or both prayers to express your praise to God for his work.

Read Psalm 92 twice, the first time to get a sense of what the psalm is saying and the ways it parallels the lives of Anna and Simeon, and the second time slowly, praying the words.

# 3

# A Prayer of Jesus

## *Praying for Christian Unity*

### John 17:1-26

I had a significant *aha* moment the summer I turned seventeen. I had been elected treasurer of the student council at my high school, and before the school year started, I went to a weeklong summer camp with all the other new student council members. At the camp, I expected we would learn specific skills for our new roles.

The camp did offer training for the tasks we would be performing, but to my surprise, a lot of emphasis was also placed on the relationships within the student council. I was, and still am, a very task-oriented person; when I have a task in mind, I find it hard to focus on the needs of the people around me. I can remember exactly where I was sitting during a small group discussion at that camp when I had my *aha* moment. For the first time in my life I found myself thinking, *You mean relationships are just as important as accomplishing tasks? Really? And part of our role on student council is to develop good relationships with each other? Is this really true?*

GROUP DISCUSSION. When are you tempted to neglect relationships and focus on something else? What are the kinds of things you find yourself focusing on to the detriment of people around you?

PERSONAL REFLECTION. What memories do you have of situations when you felt hurt because the people around you put more emphasis on a task, or a piece of God's truth, than the needs of people? If you have hurtful memories, write out a prayer to God, asking for God's mercy to you and for his help to let go of that memory. In your written prayer, you may also want to ask for God's help for those times when you neglect to show love to the people around you because you are focused on something else.

Jesus' prayer in John 17 for his disciples and for all the disciples who will follow after reminds us of the importance of relationships between believers—and invites us to make that a topic of prayer as well. *Read John 17:1-26.*

---

**1.** How do you think you would have felt as one of the disciples listening to Jesus' prayer?

---

**2.** What two primary concepts do verses 1 to 5 focus on?

What do you learn about both of these concepts from Jesus' words?

---

**3.** What do you think Jesus means by the word *know* in his definition of eternal life in verse 3?

---

**4.** What two requests does Jesus pray for his disciples in verses 11, 15 and 17?

Why do you think these are the two requests Jesus makes?

---

**5.** If you were to pick one of these prayers to pray for yourself, which one would it be and why?

---

**6.** In verses 20 to 26, Jesus shifts his focus to those who will believe through the disciples' message, which includes Christians throughout all time, including today. What is Jesus' central concern in this part of his prayer?

Why is that his central concern?

---

**7.** Have you seen instances where the love between Christians has helped others see Jesus more clearly? If so, explain.

---

**8.** In these verses, Jesus states directly what he wants. When you pray is it easy or hard for you to state directly what you want from God? Why?

---

**9.** How is oneness between Christians related to oneness between Jesus and his Father?

---

**10.** According to verses 20 to 26, in what ways is Jesus essential if a person wants to know God the Father?

---

**11.** If Christians all over the world prayed verses 20 to 26 regularly, what do you think might be the outcome?

**12.** What are the situations in your family, Bible study group, fellowship group, church or city for which you might pray for unity and love among Christians?

How might God want to use you to help bring about that love and unity?

*Spend some time praying for unity among Christians and that God would show you ways you could grow in loving your Christian brothers and sisters.*

## Now or Later

Read 1 John 4:7-12, another passage that emphasizes the love that God desires Christians to have for each other. Turn the passage in 1 John into a prayer and pray it for the Christians in your family, small group, church, neighborhood or workplace.

Read Psalm 133, noting the ways it parallels Jesus' concerns in his prayer. Then read the psalm a second time, praying that God would make it true in your family, small group, church or other Christian community.

# 4

# A Prayer of Jesus

## *Submitting to God's Will*

**Matthew 26:36-46**

Like many people, I do not enjoy conflict. I can remember several times in my life when God seemed to be directing me very clearly to say something to a friend or colleague that he or she wouldn't like to hear. One time a friend was engaging in behavior that I thought was wrong; another time a coworker hurt me very deeply. In both instances I felt God's urging to say something to the other person.

I really, really did not want to have those conversations! But as I prayed, asking God whether he truly did want me to speak up, I continued to feel led to say something. Finally I did. My words didn't make huge changes in my friend's life or in my colleague's behavior, but I did speak honestly and, I hope, lovingly. I can look back and feel grateful that I obeyed God. I can also see that those kinds of conversations come somewhat more easily to me now because I have had some practice.

GROUP DISCUSSION. Have you ever felt led by God to do something that you really didn't want to do? Do you remember wrestling with God in prayer about it? Describe what you learned from that situation.

PERSONAL REFLECTION. If you are feeling led by God to do something you don't want to do right now, write out a prayer that expresses your concerns about the situation as well as your willingness to try to obey. Or write out a prayer expressing your willingness to obey God even when God leads you to do something you don't want to do.

Jesus wrestled with his Father in the garden of Gethsemane, praying his willingness to obey God. We are privileged to have a glimpse into that sacred conversation that helps us see how honesty in prayer transforms us into willing servants of God. *Read Matthew 26:36-46.*

---

**1.** Verses 36 to 39 lay out the characters and the setting. If you were staging this scene for a play, where would you put the people on the stage?

What kinds of props and lighting would you use?

---

**2.** In verses 37 and 38, what words would you use to describe the emotions Jesus is experiencing?

**3.** How does it make you feel to read about the intensity of Jesus' emotions?

---

**4.** Note that Jesus prays "with his face to the ground" (v. 39). Why do you think he prays this way?

---

**5.** Paraphrase Jesus' prayer in verse 39. What is he saying and why?

---

**6.** Sleep is often used figuratively in the Bible to represent mental or spiritual lethargy—being dull, slow or sluggish. Why does Jesus emphasize to the disciples the importance of staying alert (vv. 40-41)?

In what ways does the disciples' sleep—their dullness and sluggishness—make Jesus' agony more intense?

**7.** Jesus' second prayer (v. 42) is slightly different than his first one (v. 39). Compare and contrast the two prayers.

What do you think caused the differences?

---

**8.** Why do you think Jesus prays the prayer a third time (v. 44)?

---

**9.** When you read Jesus' words in verses 45 and 46, what tone of voice do you imagine him using?

What do you perceive to be his mood at this point in the story?

---

**10.** How has Jesus' mood shifted over the course of this incident?

**11.** Jesus expresses his desire not to have to suffer and die on the cross, but also his willingness to do what his Father wants him to do. Why are both of these components important in prayer?

---

**12.** In what areas of your life are you most likely to need to pray a prayer like Jesus' prayer?

*Spend some time asking God to help you come to prayer with honesty and with a willingness to obey.*

**Now or Later**

The Lord's Prayer is the most famous of Jesus' prayers. Read Matthew 6:5-15 and notice Jesus' words that precede and follow the Lord's Prayer. Which instructions of Jesus are most important for you to remember as you pray?

Read Psalm 139:1-12. Consider the comfort this psalm can give in agonizing situations like Jesus experienced in the garden. Read the psalm slowly a second time, praying the words for yourself and for anyone you know who feels far away from God.

# 5

# A Prayer of Peter

## *Discussion with God*

### *Acts 10:1-33*

In my early twenties, I was in a Bible study group with three other women. One of them often talked about hearing God speak to her. She liked to take walks to pray, and she often heard God's voice in the midst of those prayer walks. I can remember asking her countless questions about how she knew it was God's voice, how she had learned to hear it and how the voice came to her. I desperately wanted to hear God speak to me. There were so many areas in my life where I longed to hear his voice.

In the years since then, I have heard God speak many times, most often to ask me to show care for someone in need. God's voice usually comes in unexpected ways at unexpected times, urging me to do something I wasn't thinking about at all. Often his voice comes while I'm praying; sometimes it also comes when I'm reading the Bible or talking with a friend. It can be an inner nudging or clear words. There are still so many areas in my life where I long to hear God's voice, but I am more confident now that I will hear what I need to hear.

GROUP DISCUSSION. On a piece of paper, write down those areas of your life where you would love to hear God speak. Then complete this sentence, "If I could hear one thing from God, I wish it would be . . ." Describe to the group one of the things you wrote on your paper.

PERSONAL REFLECTION. Have you experienced God's voice speaking to you? Does his voice come to you most often in prayer? when you read the Scriptures? in conversations with others? in expected or unexpected ways? Write out a prayer asking God to open the ears of your heart to hear his voice more readily. In the prayer, express your willingness to obey God when he does speak to you.

Peter learns an important truth as he dialogues with God in prayer, revealing how much can be learned when we speak *and* listen in our own times of prayer. *Read Acts 10:1-33.*

---

**1.** If this passage were a short story in an anthology, what title would you give it?

---

**2.** What do you learn about Cornelius in verses 1 to 8?

**3.** What adjectives would you use to describe Cornelius's response to the angel (vv. 4, 7, 8)?

---

**4.** If an angel appeared to you and asked you to do something totally unexpected, what do you imagine your response would be?

---

**5.** Describe Peter's reactions during his vision and immediately after it.

---

**6.** Why do you think Peter reacts the ways he does?

---

**7.** The dialogue between God and Peter is repeated three times (vv. 13-16). What does God's dialogue with Peter reveal about God?

**8.** Over the course of the actions in verses 19 to 29, Peter comes to understand that the vision from God that he received was not really about food at all. What key truth does Peter eventually realize about God and humans?

---

**9.** Go back over the whole story, looking for the role of prayer in this sequence of events. Can you picture this event happening without Cornelius's and Peter's prayers? Why or why not?

---

**10.** Identify the places in this passage where Cornelius and Peter choose to be obedient. How much do they know about each situation when they choose to obey?

What is still unknown to them when they choose to obey?

---

**11.** In your life or in other people's lives, how have you seen a regular practice of prayer make someone ready to hear God's voice and more likely to obey?

**12.** Have you experienced, or seen someone else experience, an argument with God? In what ways is an argument with God the sign of a healthy relationship with him?

*Spend some time praying for openness to hear God's voice and courage to obey what you hear.*

## Now or Later

Acts 13:1-3 describes a group of Christians who were praying and fasting when they heard God's voice directing them to do something unexpected. Read the passage and write out a prayer telling God how you feel about hearing his voice.

Is there something in your life right now that you feel God nudging you to do, but you're having trouble obeying? If so, commit to dialoguing with God about it each day this week, speaking and listening for his voice. Ask your small group or a friend to pray for you as well—that you'd be faithful to obey.

Read Psalm 119:33-35, observing the themes of listening and obedience that parallel the story of Cornelius and Peter. Then read the verses slowly a second time, praying them to indicate your willingness to listen to God and obey him.

# 6

# A Prayer of Paul

## *Becoming Rooted in God's Love*

### *Ephesians 3:7-21*

Wes is a hospital chaplain, and he loves his job. He considers it a great honor to be present in those holy moments when patients and loved ones wrestle with their mortality, think about what really matters to them and come face to face with God.

He can tell countless stories about people who rediscovered the power of prayer while in the hospital and has had the privilege of walking with people as they reclaimed the faith they had as children. He has also seen relatives reconcile after years of feuding.

"Money can't buy this stuff," he says when he reflects on the miracles he has seen in hospital rooms. He feels like a rich man because he gets to see God's presence there.

GROUP DISCUSSION. What are the settings in your life where you experience spiritual riches in Christ? Describe to the group what those riches feel like to you.

PERSONAL REFLECTION. When do you feel spiritually rich in Christ? What stifles that awareness of having spiritual riches in Christ? In what ways would you like to experience

Christ's riches more fully? Write a prayer asking for God's help in this area.

The apostle Paul understands the riches we have in Christ and prays for the Christians in Ephesus to receive those same riches. His prayer gives us wonderful examples of requests we can make of God on behalf of brothers and sisters in the body of Christ. *Read Ephesians 3:7-21.*

---

**1.** What emotions do you sense behind Paul's words in this prayer?

---

**2.** According to verses 7 to 11, what is God's intent?

What is his purpose?

---

**3.** What do you think Paul means by "the unsearchable riches of Christ"?

**4.** What are some actions we can take in our everyday lives to help us become more aware of these riches that are ours as Christ's followers?

---

**5.** Verse 12 says that we can approach God with freedom and confidence because of Christ. What do you think are the greatest impediments to approaching God with freedom and confidence?

---

**6.** Describe the role played by each of the three persons of the Trinity—Father, Son and Holy Spirit—in verses 14 to 21.

---

**7.** Verses 16 to 19 contain two distinct requests. Summarize each of the two requests.

Power is mentioned twice in these two requests. Why is God's power necessary to make them happen in our lives?

**8.** Do you think "inner being" and "heart" in verses 16 and 17 refer to the same thing or to something different? Why?

---

**9.** Verse 17 draws on two metaphors: a building or home (Christ dwelling in our hearts and being established in love), and a plant or tree (being rooted in love). How do these two metaphors further your understanding of Paul's desires for the Ephesians?

---

**10.** How can we know something that surpasses knowledge (v. 19)?

---

**11.** In the doxology in verses 20 and 21, the word "power" is used for the fourth time in this passage we are studying (vv. 7, 16, 18, 20). "Glory" ("glorious" in v. 16) is used for the third time (vv. 13, 16, 21). In what ways are God's power and glory connected?

---

**12.** If you could pick one part of this prayer to pray for yourself or someone else, what would it be and why?

*Read verses 14 to 19 as a prayer, either aloud or silently, praying Paul's words as you read, asking for these words to be true for yourself and for others in your life.*

## Now or Later

Ephesians 1:15-19, Paul's prayer in the first chapter of his letter to the Ephesians, has similar themes to the prayer in chapter 3. Read the prayer in chapter 1, looking for the similarities and differences with the prayer in chapter 3. Pray the words of this prayer for yourself.

Read Psalm 36:5-10, looking for the ways the passage parallels the themes of Paul's prayer. Read it slowly a second time, praising God using the words of the psalm and asking God to make his love more real in your life and in the lives of those you care about.

# 7

# A Prayer of Paul

## *Asking God for Wisdom*

### Colossians 1:1-14

Gardeners often talk about what they learn from growing plants and from the soil, the weather and the wind. Christians who garden understand and experience the many metaphors in the Bible that refer to plants and fruit bearing.

Gardening teaches patience. It requires planning. Things that are done in the early stages—such as composting, preparing the soil and making sure that a source of water is available—will have a significant impact months or even years later when the flowers and fruit appear.

In the life of faith, things that are done in the early stages—believing in the gospel of Christ, striving to know God's will, and absorbing spiritual wisdom and understanding through studying the Bible and learning from older Christians—will also have an impact months and years later, when the fruit appears.

GROUP DISCUSSION. Have you ever experienced fruit in your life from a decision or practice that took place much earlier? Describe what happened.

PERSONAL REFLECTION. Look back on your life and make a chart of decisions and choices that you can now see are significant. This might include turning points, major or minor decisions, times of commitment or dedication to an endeavor. What fruit do you see now from those moments in the past? Spend some time thanking God for the items on your chart.

In his prayer in Colossians 1, the apostle Paul asks that God will give the Colossian Christians knowledge of God's will so that they can live a life worthy of the Lord and bear fruit in good works. His prayer offers us new ways to pray for other believers. *Read Colossians 1:1-14.*

---

**1.** Imagine you are one of the Colossian Christians. How do you think you would have felt after reading this first part of Paul's letter?

Does knowing someone is praying for you make a difference? Why or why not?

---

**2.** In verses 3 to 8, Paul expresses his gratitude to God for the Colossians. What characteristics of the Colossians is he thankful for?

**3.** What do you learn about the gospel from Paul's words in verses 3 to 8?

---

**4.** According to Paul, how is the Colossians' faith and love connected to the gospel?

---

**5.** Do you think believing in the gospel always results in the kind of faith and love Paul sees in the Colossians? Why or why not?

---

**6.** In verses 9 to 12 Paul prays for the Colossians. List the components of his prayer.

How are these components related to each other?

---

**7.** In what ways do you think knowledge, wisdom and understanding are similar in meaning?

In what ways do you think they're different?

---

**8.** What is the purpose of power (v. 11)?

---

**9.** In verses 6 and 10 the metaphor of bearing fruit is used. What characteristics of growing fruit are relevant to the central themes of this prayer?

---

**10.** Near the end of the prayer, in verse 12, Paul prays that the Colossians would be thankful. Why do you think he includes thankfulness in the prayer?

What relationship do you see between thankfulness and fruitfulness in your own life?

---

**11.** How does this prayer encourage you to pray in new ways for family members, friends and other people you care about?

*Spend some time praying for people you are concerned about, using part or all of Paul's prayer.*

## Now or Later

In Philippians 1:3-11, the apostle Paul prays for the Christians in Philippi. Many of the themes of this prayer are similar to the themes of Paul's prayer in Colossians 1. Read Paul's prayer in Philippians 1, looking for those similarities. Note the differences as well. Read the prayer from Philippians a second time, praying the words for someone in your life who needs this prayer.

Read Psalm 1, the first time slowly to get an overview of the psalm and to see the parallels with Paul's prayer, and the second time as a prayer for fruitfulness for yourself or for someone you love.

# 8

# John's Vision

## *Praying with Our Bodies*

### *Revelation 1:9-20*

I was raised in Episcopal and Anglican churches, so I've had a lot of experience kneeling to pray and to receive Communion. I have always appreciated that feeling of humility and submission that comes from receiving Communion on my knees.

A number of years ago, I realized that some people use their bodies in prayer in creative ways that go beyond kneeling. I was leading a worship service at a women's retreat and, to my surprise, many of the younger women cupped their hands as I said the words of the benediction. It looked like they wanted to catch those words and hold onto them.

Perhaps they always cupped their hands like that on Sunday mornings at church, but I had never noticed. After that retreat, I began paying attention to the way people, particularly in the younger generations, used their bodies in worship. I saw a variety of hand motions and positions that paralleled the words of prayers and songs. I also saw people kneeling at unexpected times in the worship service, swaying in time with the music and sometimes even dancing in the aisles.

GROUP DISCUSSION. List the ways you have used your body in prayer and worship. What emotions and inner attitudes does each body posture communicate to you? Are there ways you would like to express aspects of prayer and worship with your body, but are unable to?

PERSONAL REFLECTION. Spend some time moving your body, experimenting with positions of your hands, arms and whole body. Observe the inner experience that accompanies the outer movement. How are these inner experiences related to prayer?

A powerful vision causes John to use his whole body in worship. John's prayerful response to the vision can inform the way we pray and help us to use our bodies more comfortably as we come before the Lord. *Read Revelation 1:9-20.*

---

**1.** If you were going to create a piece of art based on what John saw, what medium would you choose and why?

What colors would you use?

---

**2.** How does John describe himself and his situation (vv. 9-10)?

**3.** When and how have you experienced "the suffering," the "kingdom" and/or "patient endurance" as characteristics of the Christian life (v. 9)?

---

**4.** In what ways do you pray for and seek to help Christians who suffer elsewhere?

---

**5.** Of all the components of John's vision of Jesus, which are most striking to you?

---

**6.** What do you think is significant about John's physical response to this vision (v. 17)?

---

**7.** What is significant about Jesus' physical response to John (v. 17)?

**8.** Jesus gives four reasons why John does not need to be afraid (vv. 17-18). Paraphrase these reasons.

Which of these gives you the most comfort?

---

**9.** Jesus gives John a command and an explanation in verses 19 and 20. If you were John, what questions would you have after hearing Jesus' words?

---

**10.** Go back over the whole passage, looking for all the places where the five senses are evoked.

---

**11.** How would you like to engage your five senses and your body more frequently in prayer? Brainstorm the ways that could be done.

*Spend some time thanking God for your body and for each of your five senses. Ask God to help you engage your whole being in prayer and worship.*

**Now or Later**

Miriam, the sister of Moses and Aaron, led the women of Israel in a joyful dance with tambourines after God led the people of Israel through the Red Sea. Read Exodus 15:20-21. Use your body to express what you're feeling to God: fear, hope, joy, thankfulness, desire.

Read Psalm 47 and notice any connections between the psalm and John's vision. Then read the psalm a second time slowly, praying the words and praising God. When you pray the first verse, clap your hands.

Has this study on prayers of the New Testament changed your perspective on or practice of prayer? If so, how? Spend time discussing as a group what you've learned or journaling about it on your own.

# Leader's Notes

*MY GRACE IS SUFFICIENT FOR YOU. (2 COR 12:9)*

Leading a Bible discussion can be an enjoyable and rewarding experience. But it can also be scary especially if you've never done it before. If this is your feeling, you're in good company. When God asked Moses to lead the Israelites out of Egypt, he replied, "O Lord, please send someone else to do it!" (Ex 4:13). It was the same with Solomon, Jeremiah and Timothy, but God helped these people in spite of their weaknesses, and he will help you as well.

You don't need to be an expert on the Bible or a trained teacher to lead a Bible discussion. The idea behind these inductive studies is that the leader guides group members to discover for themselves what the Bible has to say. This method of learning will allow group members to remember much more of what is said than a lecture would.

These studies are designed to be led easily. As a matter of fact, the flow of questions through the passage from observation to interpretation to application is so natural that you may feel that the studies lead themselves. This study guide is also flexible. You can use it with a variety of groups student, professional, neighborhood or church groups. Each study takes forty-five to sixty minutes in a group setting.

There are some important facts to know about group dynamics and encouraging discussion. The suggestions listed below should enable you to effectively and enjoyably fulfill your role as leader.

**Preparing for the Study**

1. Ask God to help you understand and apply the passage in your own life. Unless this happens, you will not be prepared to lead others. Pray too for the various members of the group. Ask God to open your hearts to the message of his Word and motivate you to action.

**2.** Read the introduction to the entire guide to get an overview of the entire book and the issues which will be explored.

**3.** As you begin each study, read and reread the assigned Bible passage to familiarize yourself with it.

**4.** This study guide is based on the New International Version of the Bible. It will help you and the group if you use this translation as the basis for your study and discussion.

**5.** Carefully work through each question in the study. Spend time in meditation and reflection as you consider how to respond.

**6.** Write your thoughts and responses in the space provided in the study guide. This will help you to express your understanding of the passage clearly.

**7.** It might help to have a Bible dictionary handy. Use it to look up any unfamiliar words, names or places. (For additional help on how to study a passage, see chapter five of *How to Lead a LifeBuilder Study*, IVP, 2018.)

**8.** Consider how you can apply the Scripture to your life. Remember that the group will follow your lead in responding to the studies. They will not go any deeper than you do.

**9.** Once you have finished your own study of the passage, familiarize yourself with the leader's notes for the study you are leading. These are designed to help you in several ways. First, they tell you the purpose the study guide author had in mind when writing the study. Take time to think through how the study questions work together to accomplish that purpose. Second, the notes provide you with additional background information or suggestions on group dynamics for various questions. This information can be useful when people have difficulty understanding or answering a question. Third, the leader's notes can alert you to potential problems you may encounter during the study.

**10.** If you wish to remind yourself of anything mentioned in the leader's notes, make a note to yourself below that question in the study.

**Leading the Study**

**1.** Begin the study on time. Open with prayer, asking God to help the group to understand and apply the passage.

**2.** Be sure that everyone in your group has a study guide. Encourage the group to prepare beforehand for each discussion by reading the introduction to the guide and by working through the questions in the study.

**3.** At the beginning of your first time together, explain that these studies are meant to be discussions, not lectures. Encourage the members of the group to participate. However, do not put pressure on those who may be hesitant to speak during the first few sessions. You may want to suggest the following guidelines to your group.

☐ Stick to the topic being discussed.

☐ Your responses should be based on the verses which are the focus of the discussion and not on outside authorities such as commentaries or speakers.

☐ These studies focus on a particular passage of Scripture. Only rarely should you refer to other portions of the Bible. This allows for everyone to participate in in-depth study on equal ground.

☐ Anything said in the group is considered confidential and will not be discussed outside the group unless specific permission is given to do so.

☐ We will listen attentively to each other and provide time for each person present to talk.

☐ We will pray for each other.

**4.** Have a group member read the introduction at the beginning of the discussion.

**5.** Every session begins with a group discussion question. The question or activity is meant to be used before the passage is read. The question introduces the theme of the study and encourages group members to begin to open up. Encourage as many members as possible to participate, and be ready to get the discussion going with your own response.

This section is designed to reveal where our thoughts or feelings need to be transformed by Scripture. That is why it is especially important not to read the passage before the discussion question is asked. The passage will tend to color the honest reactions people would otherwise give because they are, of course, supposed to think the way the Bible does.

You may want to supplement the group discussion question with an icebreaker to help people to get comfortable. See the community section of the *Small Group Starter Kit* (IVP, 1995) for more ideas.

You also might want to use the personal reflection question with your group. Either allow a time of silence for people to respond individually or discuss it together.

**6.** Have a group member (or members if the passage is long) read aloud the passage to be studied. Then give people several minutes to read the passage again silently so that they can take it all in.

**7.** Question 1 will generally be an overview question designed to briefly survey the passage. Encourage the group to look at the whole passage, but try to avoid getting sidetracked by questions or issues that will be addressed later in the study.

**8.** As you ask the questions, keep in mind that they are designed to be used just as they are written. You may simply read them aloud. Or you may prefer to express them in your own words.

There may be times when it is appropriate to deviate from the study guide. For example, a question may have already been answered. If so, move on to the next question. Or someone may raise an important question not covered in the guide. Take time to discuss it, but try to keep the group from going off on tangents.

**9.** Avoid answering your own questions. If necessary, repeat or rephrase them until they are clearly understood. Or point out something you read in the leader's notes to clarify the context or meaning. An eager group quickly becomes passive and silent if they think the leader will do most of the talking.

**10.** Don't be afraid of silence. People may need time to think about the question before formulating their answers.

**11.** Don't be content with just one answer. Ask, "What do the rest of you think?" or "Anything else?" until several people have given answers to the question.

**12.** Acknowledge all contributions. Try to be affirming whenever possible. Never reject an answer. If it is clearly off-base, ask, "Which verse led you to that conclusion?" or again, "What do the rest of you think?"

**13.** Don't expect every answer to be addressed to you, even though this will probably happen at first. As group members become more at ease, they will begin to truly interact with each other. This is one sign of healthy discussion.

**14.** Don't be afraid of controversy. It can be very stimulating. If you don't resolve an issue completely, don't be frustrated. Move on and keep it in mind for later. A subsequent study may solve the problem.

**15.** Periodically summarize what the group has said about the passage. This helps to draw together the various ideas mentioned and gives continuity to the study. But don't preach.

**16.** At the end of the Bible discussion you may want to allow group members a time of quiet to work on an idea under "Now or Later." Then discuss what you experienced. Or you may want to encourage group members to work on these ideas between meetings. Give an opportunity during the session for people to talk about what they are learning.

**17.** Conclude your time together with conversational prayer, adapting the prayer suggestion at the end of the study to your group. Ask for God's help in following through on the commitments you've made.

**18.** End on time.

Many more suggestions and helps are found in *How to Lead a LifeBuilder Study.*

**Components of Small Groups**

A healthy small group should do more than study the Bible. There are four components to consider as you structure your time together.

*Nurture.* Small groups help us to grow in our knowledge and love of God. Bible study is the key to making this happen and is the foundation of your small group.

*Community.* Small groups are a great place to develop deep friendships with other Christians. Allow time for informal interaction before and after each study. Plan activities and games that will help you get to know each other. Spend time having fun together going on a picnic or cooking dinner together.

*Worship and prayer.* Your study will be enhanced by spending time praising God together in prayer or song. Pray for each other's needs and keep track of how God is answering prayer in your group. Ask God to help you to apply what you are learning in your study.

*Outreach.* Reaching out to others can be a practical way of applying what you are learning, and it will keep your group from becoming self-focused. Host a series of evangelistic discussions for your friends or neighbors. Clean up the yard of an elderly friend. Serve at a soup kitchen together, or spend a day working in the community.

Many more suggestions and helps in each of these areas are found in the *Small Group Starter Kit.* You will also find information on building a small group. Reading through the starter kit will be worth your time.

**Study 1. A Prayer of Mary: Praising the Mighty One. Luke 1:39-56.**

*Purpose:* To grow in prayer, both praise and intercession, based on God's power and his willingness to intervene in our lives.

**General note.** Mary and Elizabeth are cousins, and both are pregnant with miracle babies. The story of Elizabeth's pregnancy is told in Luke

1:5-25, and the story of the birth of her son, John the Baptist, is told in Luke 1:57-80. Mary's visit by the angel, announcing that she would bear a son miraculously, is described in Luke 1:26-38. Mary's prayer in Luke 1:46-55 is known as the Magnificat, because that is the first word of the prayer in Latin.

**Question 2.** *Blessed* is often used in the Bible to refer to God, where it conveys praise of God. *Blessed* is also used to refer to people. In those instances it means happy, fortunate, favored or joyful; these characteristics come from God's grace and goodness in people's lives.

**Question 3.** The combination of "Savior" and "Mighty One" as names for God in this prayer is worthy of note. "Savior" conveys God's personal care for our need, and "Mighty One" evokes power and success in battle. This combination of power and personal care for humans is one of the central themes of Mary's prayer. The addition of the word "holy" (v. 49) implies that God's power and personal care will be used in our lives for things that are good and right.

**Questions 5-6.** The word *fear* is used throughout the Bible to express one aspect of a good and healthy relationship with God. In the Bible, to fear God is to revere God, desire to obey his commands and be willing to turn away from evil. The fear of God is portrayed in the Bible as the beginning of wisdom. At the same time, the New Testament is clear that we do not need to be afraid of God, because God's love and forgiveness are made visible in Jesus Christ. Still, holy fear, in the sense of reverence, is appropriate and desirable in God's eyes.

**Question 7.** Reversals are central to the story of the Bible. In the Old Testament, God chose Abraham to be the father of the people of Israel, and through this small nation, God intended to bless all the nations of the earth. The biggest reversal is the death and resurrection of Jesus. Through submitting to a humiliating death, Jesus conquered death and brought eternal life to his followers.

**Question 10.** In a commentary on this passage, François Bovon writes, "Luke wants to say something about *God* with the Magnificat. The song extols the threefold activity of God on the religious, sociopolitical, and ethnic levels. As Lord and God, he is transcendent, stands on the side of the poor, and applies his work to all of humanity through Israel. I see in it the God who lays claim to the whole of a human life, and places his power in the service of his compassion" (*Luke 1: A Commentary on the Gospel of Luke 1:1—9:50,* ed. Helmut Koester, trans. Christine M. Thomas, Hermeneia [Minneapolis: Fortress, 2002], pp. 64, 65).

**Study 2. Prayers of Simeon and Anna: Seeing God at Work. Luke 2:22-38.**

*Purpose:* To see the role of obedience and sensitivity to God's Holy Spirit in enabling us to praise and thank God.

**General note.** Simeon's prayer is known as the Nunc Dimittis, because those are the first two words of his prayer in Latin.

**Group discussion.** You should have paper and pens or pencils on hand for this opening question.

**Question 2.** By bringing an offering of two doves or pigeons, Mary and Joseph are obeying God's commands in Leviticus 12:1-8, and by presenting Jesus in the temple, Mary and Joseph are obeying Exodus 13:2, 12-16. These actions indicate that Mary and Joseph are faithful and obedient to God's Law and that they are not wealthy enough to afford a lamb for the offering. Later in his life, when Jesus argued with the religious leaders about the Law, he did so as an insider who had been raised by parents who were meticulously faithful in observing it.

**Question 5.** The verb *dismiss* can be a way of euphemistically describing death, or it can refer to the liberation of a slave or servant from service. In this prayer, it probably refers to death. The present tense may indicate that Simeon is aware that he will die soon. He knows he can die with joy in his heart because God has permitted him to see the One who will bring salvation to the Jews and also to the whole world. Simeon's prayer is a part of the ancient Compline service—an evening service—because evening, when light is waning, is the time of day most like death.

**Question 6.** In Jesus' time, the people of Israel expected a Messiah to come to free them from Roman oppression. The Old Testament contains many indications that God cares for the salvation of the whole world (Gentiles and Jews), but by Jesus' time the people of Israel had narrowed their expectations to focus on their occupation by Rome. This is completely understandable in an occupied and oppressed nation, but it makes Simeon's prayer all the more remarkable. God's concern in salvation goes far beyond one nation in terrible circumstances, and God's liberation addresses human need in every part of the earth and in every form of slavery to sin and death.

**Question 7.** While it is unusual for a woman to be called a prophetess, four women in the Old Testament are given that designation: Miriam (Ex 15:20), Deborah (Judg 4:4), Huldah (2 Kings 22:14) and Isaiah's wife (Is 8:3).

**Question 9.** Anna's and Simeon's lifetime of obedience enabled them to see God at work in this little baby who had been brought by Joseph and Mary to the temple. Their years of obeying God and their openness to the Holy Spirit enabled them to pray the prayers that are recorded or described here. At the same time, their prayers over the years probably played a role in their ability to obey God and remain open to the Spirit. Many Christians report that obedience, prayer and openness to the Spirit fuel each other and build on each other. Each one helps make the other ones possible.

**Study 3. A Prayer of Jesus: Praying for Christian Unity. John 17:1-26.**

*Purpose:* To learn about Jesus' priorities as he prays for his disciples and for all Christians.

**General note.** The setting for this prayer is Jesus' last night with his disciples, right before his betrayal and death. This prayer is often called Jesus' high priestly prayer, a reference to Jesus' sacrificial death, which is imminent. This is the longest recorded prayer of Jesus.

**Question 2.** The first five verses focus on eternal life and glory. "Glory" in the Hebrew worldview comes from the root idea of heaviness, weight and worthiness. In the secular Greek world it meant reputation or opinion. Here, glory means all of that, and also has an interesting relational component to it, with the Father and Son giving each other glory.

**Question 3.** In the Jewish mindset, to "know" is much more than the cognitive, detached or objective knowledge that we talk about in our world. Knowing, as used in the Bible, involves experience and intimacy and includes our whole lives.

**Question 4.** "Sanctify" in verse 17 means to set apart for sacred use or to make holy.

**Question 6.** Jesus' disciples, for whom he was praying earlier in this prayer, are the ones who will write or influence the books of the New Testament, and they are the ones who will spread the Christian gospel throughout the Roman world. Because of them, we can have faith today. Truly, we are the ones who believe because of the disciples' message.

**Question 11.** Scholars and church leaders have engaged in long discussions about what the unity that Jesus prays for would look like in real life. Would Jesus have desired no separate churches and denominations? The New Testament affirms the significance of diversity (1 Cor 12:4-7) in expressions of faith alongside unity of love for God and for each other. So it is interesting to discuss the question of what unity and love look like when accompanied by a diversity of gifts, ways of serving and expressions of faith.

**Study 4. A Prayer of Jesus: Submitting to God's Will. Matthew 26:36-46.**

*Purpose:* To grow in willingness to be honest with God and, at the same time, obey God.

**General note.** This incident takes place on the last night of Jesus' life. He knows that he is going to be betrayed and sentenced to death.

Matthew refers several times to the disciples James and John as the "sons of Zebedee." Also, Gethsemane means "oil press." Scholars are not sure of the exact location of the garden of Gethsemane, but they agree that it was probably located east of Jerusalem, across the Kidron Valley from the temple mount, on or near the Mount of Olives. The modern-day garden of Gethsemane may or may not be the original location.

**Question 5.** The word *cup* is used figuratively throughout the Bible to mean one of two things: (1) a person's divinely appointed destiny or (2) the share of blessings or disasters allotted to a person. In this instance it seems to refer to the destiny that the Father had appointed for Jesus, to die on the cross for the salvation of human beings.

**Question 6.** Jesus "expresses pained surprise that these three able-bodied fisherman, who had spent many sleepless nights toiling alone on the Sea of Galilee, are so lacking in strength that they cannot keep awake with Him for a single hour. . . . They had all three shown themselves to be eager and impetuous . . . but without the discipline and strength of prayer the human spirit, Jesus reminds them, is all too easily overcome by the impulses of the flesh" (R. V. G. Tasker, *The Gospel According to Matthew,* Tyndale New Testament Commentaries [Leicester, U.K.: Inter-Varsity Press, 1961], p. 249).

**Question 7.** The second prayer, with its negative construction ("if it is not possible . . .") may indicate that Jesus is more resigned to his task than he was earlier.

**Question 10.** Donald A. Hagner writes about Jesus after he has prayed: "While the disciples in their sleepy stupor remain uncomprehending, for Jesus the immediate crisis is over and the final act about to begin. Now unwaveringly his face is set toward the cross and the fulfillment of his Father's will" (*Matthew 14—28,* Word Biblical Commentary, vol. 33b [Nashville: Thomas Nelson, 1995], p. 785).

**Question 11.** Many Christians believe it is not spiritual to express our desires. Jesus models an entirely appropriate way of expressing what we feel and think. He says what he wants, and he says he is willing to obey God in spite of what he wants. The weight of Jesus' sorrow and sadness, and his honesty in coming before God in the midst of his sorrow, is a wonderful model for us, particularly when it is coupled with his willingness to obey.

**Study 5. A Prayer of Peter: Discussion with God. Acts 10:1-33.**
*Purpose:* To grow in willingness to hear God's voice and engage in dialogue with God.
**Group discussion.** Be sure to have paper and pens or pencils on hand for this question.
**Question 2.** Cornelius, as a Roman soldier, is not a Jew. He is a Gentile, and Jews did not socialize with Gentiles because they considered them to be unclean. A Roman centurion was the rough equivalent of an Army captain today. A centurion had one hundred soldiers under him. Caesarea was the Roman capital of the province of Judea. Like Joppa (called Jaffa today), Caesarea is set on the Mediterranean Sea, about thirty miles north of Joppa. Therefore walking between them would probably take two days. At 3 p.m., Cornelius might have been praying, because 3:00 was a traditional time for prayer.
**Question 5.** The Jews had very specific laws about which animals, birds, insects, lizards and fish were appropriate for food and which ones were not permitted. (They were called "clean" and "unclean" foods; see Lev 11:1-47 and Deut 14:3-21.) Since the sheet contained "all kinds of" animals, reptiles and birds, it must have contained a mix of clean and unclean foods.
**Question 6.** The emotional impact of this passage may be hard to understand for many Christians today. Anthony B. Robinson and Robert W. Wall, writing from an American point of view, note that when Peter sees the animals and hears God's word to eat them, it is "perhaps difficult for most contemporary people to fully appreciate Peter's instinctive revulsion, since the ideal of unclean or taboo foods is not common among contemporary Christians. Still, we might get some idea of his emotion if we were to visit China, say, and were offered a dish of roast dog or rat; or if, in Japan, we were invited to eat fish or other sea life that was still alive and wriggling" (*Called to Be Church: The Book of Acts for a New Day* [Grand Rapids: Eerdmans, 2006], p. 162).

**Question 8.** Peter explains in verse 28 exactly what he learned from the experience: "God has shown me that I should not call any man impure or unclean." These are remarkable, even radical, words for a faithful Jew who had probably never been in the home of a Gentile and who had most likely never considered that God would answer the prayers of a Gentile. One helpful way to understand Peter's transformation is to imagine the conversation on the two-day trip between Joppa and Caesarea. Cornelius's servants and the soldier he sent probably talked about their master, giving Peter an understanding of Cornelius's upright character and his hunger for God. In addition, Peter may have discussed his vision with the brothers from Joppa who accompanied him, and in talking it over may have grown in understanding God's purposes in the events that were happening.

**Study 6. A Prayer of Paul: Becoming Rooted in God's Love. Ephesians 3:7-21.**

*Purpose:* To grow in ability to pray for God's love to be poured out in the lives of others.

**General note.** A prayer from the Syrian Clementine Liturgy, which may date back as far as the fourth century, has some of the same themes as Paul's prayer. It uses different metaphors than Paul's prayer, but shows that humans often need to draw on the power of metaphors to express the abundance of God's love in our finite language: "O God, the unsearchable abyss of peace, the ineffable sea of love, the fountain of blessings and the bestower of affection, who sends peace to those who receive it, open to us this day the sea of your love, and water us with plenteous streams from the riches of your grace and the most sweet springs of your benignity" (Thomas C. Oden and Cindy Crosby, *Ancient Christian Devotional: Lectionary Cycle A* [Downers Grove, Ill.: InterVarsity Press, 2007], p. 160).

**Question 3.** In the New Testament, material riches are often viewed as a hindrance to Christian living, such as in the story of the rich young ruler in Mark 10:17-25. In that encounter, Jesus says that it is hard for those who are materially rich to enter the kingdom of God, but he encourages the young man to give away his possessions to gain "treasure in heaven" (Mk 10:21). Elsewhere Jesus uses the phrase "rich toward God" (Lk 12:21), which seems to be a close parallel to the "unsearchable riches of Christ" (Eph 3:8) and God's "glorious riches" which comes later in Ephesians 3:16. Based on what Paul has written in Ephesians 1, he may be using "glorious riches" in 3:16 to refer to all the ways God has blessed us in Christ, giving us love, wisdom, knowledge, an inheritance and a destiny.

**Question 6.** It is very rare to find all three persons of the Trinity in a passage in the Bible. Another passage where all three persons of the Trinity are represented is at Jesus' baptism. In the first centuries after Christ, when the leaders of the early church were trying to articulate the doctrine of the Trinity, they examined the Bible carefully to tease out the roles played by each person of the Trinity. In this passage, the actions attributed to the Father, Son and Holy Spirit are not designed to be a systematic presentation of everything God does, working through the three persons of the Trinity, but it is still very interesting to note which actions Paul attributes to each.

**Question 7.** The apostle Paul was very concerned about power. The word "power" is used eight times in Ephesians and fifty-six times in the letters attributed to Paul. His letters make clear that it is not enough to give intellectual assent to the truths of the Christian faith. To him, it is only by God's power that we can enter into relationship with God and experience God's love. God's power is absolutely necessary for us to live a life of faith, free from the bondage to sin and evil. We human beings so easily slide into the belief that we do things by ourselves. A serious reflection on the role of God's power can help us grow in understanding our dependence on God.

**Question 8.** Commentators disagree about whether "inner being" and "heart" refer to the same thing, so a discussion about the meanings attached to these words can be helpful and interesting. Some of the possible ways to think about the heart and/or inner being are identity, vitality, will, intelligence, real self, decision-making apparatus, and center of our spiritual and psychological life.

Throughout much of Christian history, Christians have been tempted to place so much emphasis on the inner being that the physical body (which we could perhaps call our "outer being") was viewed as irrelevant or even a hindrance to faith. That view lingers in some settings today, and it results in a lack of care and respect for our bodies. However, the secular culture currently seems intent on emphasizing the opposite view, that physical beauty and fitness are all that matters. A healthy Christian view emphasizes both the nurture of faith in the inner being and careful stewardship of the outer being.

**Question 9.** The two metaphors used in verse 17—God dwelling with us and us being rooted in God like a tree—are used elsewhere in the Bible as well. Paul speaks of "Christ in you" (Col 1:27) and says "Christ lives in me" (Gal 2:20). John uses the language of Christ making his home with us (Jn 14:23). Psalm 1 and Jeremiah 17:7-8 portray the person who loves God as a tree planted by streams of water.

Love for God and love for people go hand in hand. As we grow to love God more, our love for the people around us will flourish, and as we love people, our heart opens up and we are more likely to be able to receive God's love. The opposite is also true. Bitterness, unresolved anger and ill will for people block our ability to grow in our love for God, and anger at God often flows over into our relationships with those around us.

**Question 10.** The Hebrew view of knowledge was as an entry point into relationship. This kind of knowledge creates demands not only on our understanding but also on our will. This verse, then, refers not to a cognitive understanding of God's love, but to God's invitation to engage in relationship with the source of love, God himself.

**Question 11.** As noted in study three, question two, "glory" in the Hebrew worldview comes from the root idea of heaviness, weight and worthiness. In the secular Greek world it meant reputation or opinion.

**Study 7. A Prayer of Paul: Asking God for Wisdom. Colossians 1:1-14.**

*Purpose:* To grow in ability to pray for wisdom and fruitfulness for others.

**Question 3.** Epaphras was a colleague of Paul's who evangelized the area around Colosse and planted churches in Colosse, Hierapolis and Laodicea. He later visited Paul in prison in Rome, and his news about the church in Colosse prompted Paul to write this letter. All that we know about Epaphras comes from Colossians 1:7; 4:12; and Philemon 23.

**Question 4.** Based on this passage, and indeed the whole New Testament, it is impossible to imagine that someone could receive the gospel and live an unchanged life. The gospel comes to us with the power to change our lives and with the call to become more like Jesus. When we receive the gospel, our ability to love increases, we grow in faith and faithfulness, and our lives bear fruit that comes from that love and faith.

**Question 6.** Paul begins by praying that the Colossians would be filled with the knowledge of God's will. This leads to living a life worthy of God, pleasing God and bearing fruit in good works, which in turn leads to increased knowledge of God. The prayer continues with more requests, but this sequence in verses 9 and 10 is worthy of note. Often we long for knowledge of God, and this sequence indicates that as we obey what we know and bear fruit, we will increase in the knowledge of God. This is a kind of knowledge that results from obedience, not knowledge that is cognitive only.

**Question 7.** In our contemporary world, knowledge is often viewed as factual information, while wisdom is viewed as knowing how to apply or use facts. In the ancient Jewish world, both knowledge and wisdom were rooted in relationship, in this case relationship with God. Both were intensely practical. While we might view knowledge or wisdom as the basis for clear thinking, in Paul's worldview wisdom and knowledge formed the foundation for appropriate action. Ultimately, then, the source of wisdom and knowledge for Paul is Christ's death and resurrection that rescued us from death and sin, and wisdom and knowledge will motivate us to act appropriately in response to Jesus' gift of life.

**Question 8.** In the note for question seven in study six, Paul's frequent use of the word "power" in his letters is mentioned. In this instance, it is noteworthy that the purpose of having God's power in our lives is to be able to have endurance and patience, so we can joyfully give thanks in all circumstances. God's power is not given so that we can lord it over people, impress others or get our own way.

**Study 8. John's Vision: Praying with Our Bodies. Revelation 1:9-20.**

*Purpose:* To grow in understanding the place of the five senses and the physical body in prayer.

**Question 2.** Patmos is a small island, about five miles wide by ten miles long, just under forty miles off the southwest coast of Asia Minor. The Romans sent people into exile on Patmos. Because of its isolation and small size, it required only a few guards. This is the only mention of "the Lord's Day" in the New Testament, but the early church used that term frequently to refer to Sunday, the day of Jesus' resurrection and the day they gathered for worship.

**Question 3.** It is significant that John received this vision while in exile. John's vision "comes not in some holy place in the midst of lavish divine service, but in a place of exile. . . . God appears to one of the suffering and oppressed people at a time of personal tribulation. It is that kind of God that Revelation (and for that matter the rest of the Bible) tells us about: a God who identifies with Hebrew slaves, a humiliated people in exile in Babylon, a crucified Messiah, an exiled Christian. In a place of isolation and exile, therefore, John meets Christ" (Christopher Rowland, *Revelation,*

Epworth Commentaries [London: Epworth Press, 1993], p. 59).
**Question 9.** The identification of the stars with angels would have special significance for people in the Roman Empire. "Whereas for the Hellenistic people, the stars represent fate, change, and immutable cosmic order, [John's vision] discloses that the stars relate to the church, to those small, insignificant groups of Christians in Asia Minor. They influence the world's fate and destiny because they are in the right hand of Christ" (Gerhard A. Krodel, *Revelation*, Augsburg Commentary on the New Testament [Minneapolis: Augsburg, 1989], p. 98).

---

*Lynne M. Baab is the author of the* Prayers of the Old Testament *and* Sabbath *LifeBuilder Bible Studies as well as numerous books, including* Fasting, Sabbath Keeping *and* Reaching Out in a Networked World. *A Presbyterian minister, she completed a PhD in communication at the University of Washington in 2007 and moved with her husband to Dunedin, New Zealand, where she taught pastoral theology at the University of Otago for ten years. She returned to her home city, Seattle, in 2017 and still supervises graduate students for her university in New Zealand.*